WAR MACHINES
TANKS

Simon Adams

FRANKLIN WATTS
LONDON • SYDNEY

IN ASSOCIATION WITH

IMPERIAL WAR
MUSEUM

First published in 2007 by Franklin Watts

Copyright © Franklin Watts 2007

Franklin Watts
338 Euston Road
London NW1 3BH

Franklin Watts Australia
Level 17/207 Kent Street
Sydney, NSW 2000

A CIP catalogue record for this book is available
from the British Library.

Dewey number: 623.7'4752

ISBN 978 0 7496 7166 2

Printed in China

Franklin Watts is a division of Hachette Children's Books,
an Hachette Livre UK company.

Editor: Sarah Ridley
Editor-in-chief: John Miles
Designer: Jason Billin
Art director: Jonathan Hair

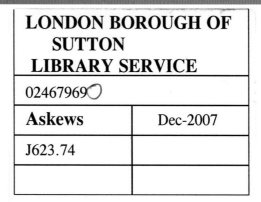
Picture credits:
All images copyright © Imperial War Museum. Cover main GLF277, bottom left QI4476, bottom middle GLF277, bottom right BL73/50/9/3; title page MH 7767; page 4 top QI4476, bottom MH7767; page 5 top R88956; page 6 top Q3551, bottom Q11696; page 7 CO3520; page 8 Q69945; page 6 top Q72558, bottom Q14642; page 10 MH19568; page 11 MH19553; page 12 STT3969; page 13 top MH4417, bottom STT2651; page 14 HU53721; page 15 top HU54923, bottom RUS2010; page 16 BU3420; page 17 top BI4423, bottom BU2743; page 18 MH8488; page 19 MH8479; page 20 B8496; page 21 top B8359, bottom B10819; page 22 MH7767; page 23 MH7794; page 24 STT9319; page 25 STT9320; page 26 top BL73/50/9/3, bottom BHQ74/137/1/7; page 27 R88956; page 28 GLF470; page 29 top GLF279, bottom GLF277; page 30-31 background Q14643

Contents

Introduction

The tank made its first appearance in 1916, during the First World War (1914–18). It was one of the most important technological inventions of the war.

The British invented the tank, and used it effectively in battle in 1917 and 1918. Tanks scared the enemy, as they could cross trenches and muddy ground, and were difficult to stop except with well-aimed artillery.

The 'water-carriers'

When the British developed the first tanks, they called them 'land ships' as they had no proper name. In order to keep their development secret, the land ships were referred to as 'water-carriers', because that is what they looked like. Even the factory workers who were making these new machines thought that they were movable tanks to contain water.

Second World War tanks

The early tanks were simple machines and often broke down. By the time of the Second World War (1939–45), tank technology had improved enormously. The new generation of tanks were speedy, highly mobile, well armed and well protected. Both sides in the war produced thousands of tanks that were used in all the major battles of the war.

Tank classification

Tanks were once classified according to their role or by their gun size or weight. Early tanks were therefore described as infantry or cruiser tanks, or light, medium and heavy tanks. Today, almost all tanks are called battle tanks, whatever their size.

In this book, we feature 12 of the most important tanks of the twentieth century. Each tank is illustrated and described in detail, with boxes listing their performance and the specifications and statistics of each model or type. A glossary at the back of the book explains any difficult words, as well as listing some interesting websites on this subject.

Mk IV

The first tank in history – the Mk 1 – was an oddly shaped box with long caterpillar tracks on either side that enabled it to grip on muddy ground and cross over defensive trenches.

The Mk 1

The Mk 1 was based on an experimental tank, nicknamed 'Little Willie', that was produced for the British army in 1915. It first saw service at the Battle of the Somme in September 1916. Many broke down, although one-third made it across enemy lines.

The Mk IV

Two training tanks – Mks II and III – were then produced before the Mk IV came into service in 1917. This version was better armoured than its predecessors and was safer for the crew. It first fought at Passchendaele in mid-1917, but proved its worth in battle at Cambrai in November 1917. Here, almost 460 tanks overcame the German trench system and advanced along a wide area for almost 9 km (5.5 miles).

▶ *The Mk IV was tested over specially built ramps and ditches.*

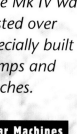

FACT FILE

★ Early tanks were produced in two versions – Male and Female – according to the guns they carried. Later versions were sexless, as they combined both Male and Female designs.

★ The crew shared the same space inside the tank as the engine. The temperature inside could rise to 50°C (122°F) and the crew often fainted or became violently sick when they breathed fresh air again.

◀ *New and old: tanks were a new invention in the First World War but they were massively outnumbered by horses, one of the oldest forms of transport.*

PERFORMANCE

Maximum road speed	5.6 km/h (3.5 mph)
Range	56 km (35 miles)

SPECS & STATS

Crew 10 – 1 commander/main driver, 1 driver/main gearbox, 2 gearsmen, 6 gunners

Width 4 m (12.8 ft) (male)   **Height** 2.5 m (8.2 ft)

Length 8 m (26.4 ft)

Weight Male: 28,400 kg (28 tons)
Female: 27,400 kg (27 tons)

Armaments Male: 2 x L23 6-pdrs, 4 x .303 Lewis MG machine guns
Female: 6 x .303 Lewis MG machine guns

Armour 6–12 mm (0.25–0.50 in)

Engine 125 hp petrol engine

Renault FT-17

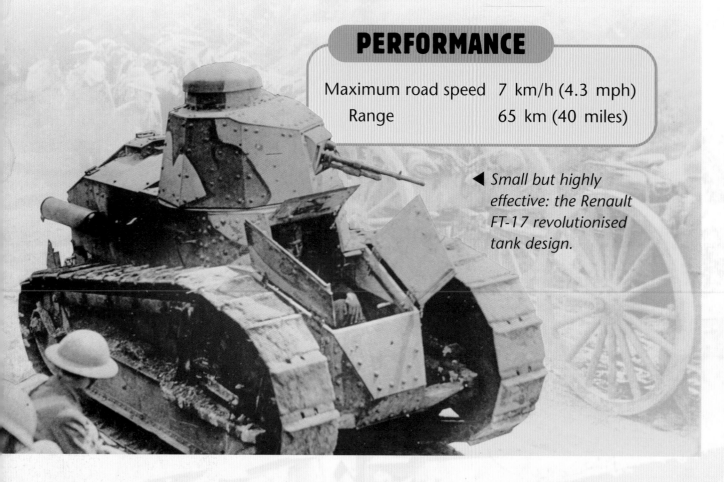

PERFORMANCE

Maximum road speed	7 km/h (4.3 mph)
Range	65 km (40 miles)

◀ *Small but highly effective: the Renault FT-17 revolutionised tank design.*

The Renault FT-17 tank might look small and even primitive to our eyes, but it is one of the most revolutionary and influential tank designs in history.

This was the first tank to have its main gun set in a fully rotating turret, and was the first to have the layout of the gun turret on top, driver in the front, and engine at the back. Almost every tank ever since has followed this simple but effective layout.

▲ *The driver and commander entered the tank through the front.*

FACT FILE

★ The 'FT' of the title does not stand for anything in particular. Every Renault model was given a combination code of letters, and this one acquired the initials FT.

★ When the Soviet Union started making tanks in the 1930s, their first tank – the T-18 – was a copy of the original Renault design with sprung suspension.

Mass-produced tank

The FT-17 came into service in early 1917. The tank was well suited to mass-production: 3,177 were delivered to the French army and another 514 direct to the US army then serving in France. After the war, thousands were made for armies in Europe and the USA. They served in the Russian, Chinese and Spanish civil wars, and even fought in the early stages of the Second World War, although by then the design was completely out of date.

SPECS & STATS

Crew	2 – commander, driver	**Width**	1.47 m (4 ft 10 in)
Height	2.14 m (7 ft)	**Length**	5 m (16 ft 5 in)
Weight	6,500 kg (6.4 tons)		
Armaments	37 mm Puteaux gun or a 7.92 mm Hotchkiss machine gun		
Armour	22 mm (0.9 in)	**Engine**	Renault 39 hp petrol engine

A7V

The vast and lumbering A7V was the only German-made tank to see action during the First World War.

It first saw action during the German offensive in eastern France on 21 March 1918 and helped to stop a minor British breakthrough in the area. One hundred of the tanks were ordered to be produced in spring 1918, but only 21 were delivered before war ended in November.

FACT FILE

★ The A7V probably stands for *Allgemeines Kriegsdepartement 7 Abteilung Verkehrswesen*, the 'General War Department 7, Branch Transportation'.

★ In German, the A7V was called a *Sturmpanzer-Kraftwagen*, or 'assault armoured motor vehicle'.

▶ *The sides of the tank covered the crawler tracks that made the tank move forwards.*

PERFORMANCE

Maximum road speed	15 km/h (9.3 mph)
Cross-country speed	5 km/h (3.1 mph)
Range	30–80 km (20–50 miles)

▲ *It's hard to tell if this is a movable tank or a stationary, fortified gun position!*

Tank versus tank

The A7V made history on 24 April 1918 when three of them took part in the first tank against tank battle in history. The three A7Vs came up against three British Mk IV tanks; one German and two British tanks were knocked out during the battle.

SPECS & STATS

Crew	18 – commander, driver, mechanic, mechanic/signaller, 12 infantrymen (6 machine gunners, 6 loaders), 2 artillerymen (main gunner, loader)
Width	3.1 m (10 ft)
Height	3.3 m (10 ft 10 in)
Length	7.34 m (24 ft 1 in)
Weight	33,000 kg (32.5 tons)
Armaments	57 mm tank gun 6 x 7.9 mm MG08/15 machine guns
Armour	20 mm (0.79 in) side armour 50 mm (2 in) front armour
Engine	2 x Daimler 4-cylinder, 100 hp engines

Panzerkampfwagen
PzKpfw III

The Panzerkampfwagen ('armoured fighting vehicle') III entered service in September 1939, right at the start of the Second World War.

Ninety-eight of these tanks took part in the German invasion of Poland, with a further 350 taking part in the invasion of the Low Countries and France in May 1940.

German fighter

This medium-weight tank was hugely effective against British and French tanks but was outclassed by the superior Soviet T-34 on the eastern front after 1942. The tank was finally withdrawn from service in 1943, by which time 5,664 had been built.

▼ A PzKpfw IIIJ. This model had an extended gun barrel.

FACT FILE

★ When this tank was first designed, it had to weigh less than 24,400 kg (24 tons), as that was the weight limit for most German road bridges.

★ After production of this tank stopped, the chassis continued to be produced for armoured infantry support vehicles armed with a 75 mm assault gun; more than 10,000 of these vehicles were built during the war.

▲ The front and rear driving sprockets had projecting cogs to grip the crawler track.

SPECS & STATS

Crew 5 – commander, driver, co-driver/hull gunner, gunner, loader

Width 2.9 m (9 ft 8 in)   **Height** 2.5 m (8 ft 3 in)

Length 6.4 m (21 ft)   **Weight** 22,300 kg (21.9 tons)

Armaments   1 x 50 mm KwK 38 L42 tank gun (late models)
                    2 x 7.92 mm MG-34 machine guns

Armour   90 mm (3.5 in) maximum

Engine   Maybach HL 120 TRM, 12-cylinder, 300 hp diesel engine

PERFORMANCE

Maximum road speed 40 km/h (25 mph)
Range   175 km (110 miles)

◀ The main gunner perched on a small seat inside the gun turret above and behind the driver.

T-34

The mainstay of the Soviet Red Army during the Second World War, the T-34 tank had the 'big three' essentials of tank design: armour, firepower and mobility.

It was designed to be mechanically simple and, above all, capable of mass-production. The first tanks rolled off the production line in 1941: by May 1944 the Soviets were turning out 1,200 T-34s a month.

An improved model

The main variant of the T-34 was the T-34–85, a major improvement on previous models. First produced in late 1943, it had a more powerful 85 mm gun and a larger turret that allowed crew numbers to increase from four to five. The commander was now freed from having to act as the main gunner and could concentrate on leading his crew and co-ordinating his action with the rest of his tank unit.

▼ *A line-up of early T-34s, ready to defend the USSR.*

PERFORMANCE

Maximum road speed	51 km/h (32 mph)
Range	360 km (225 miles)

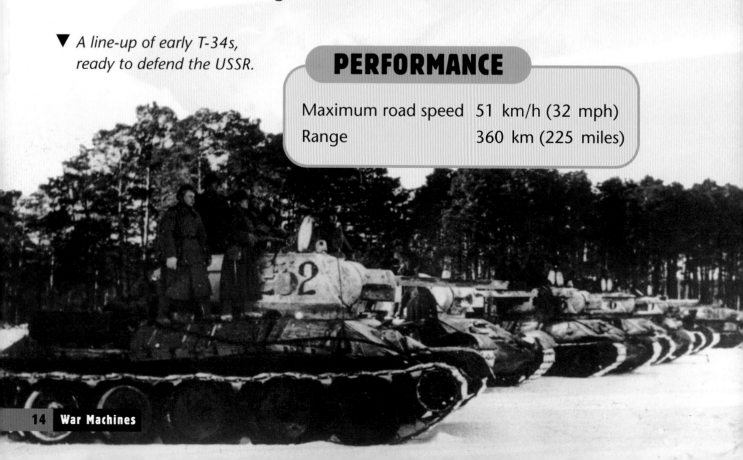

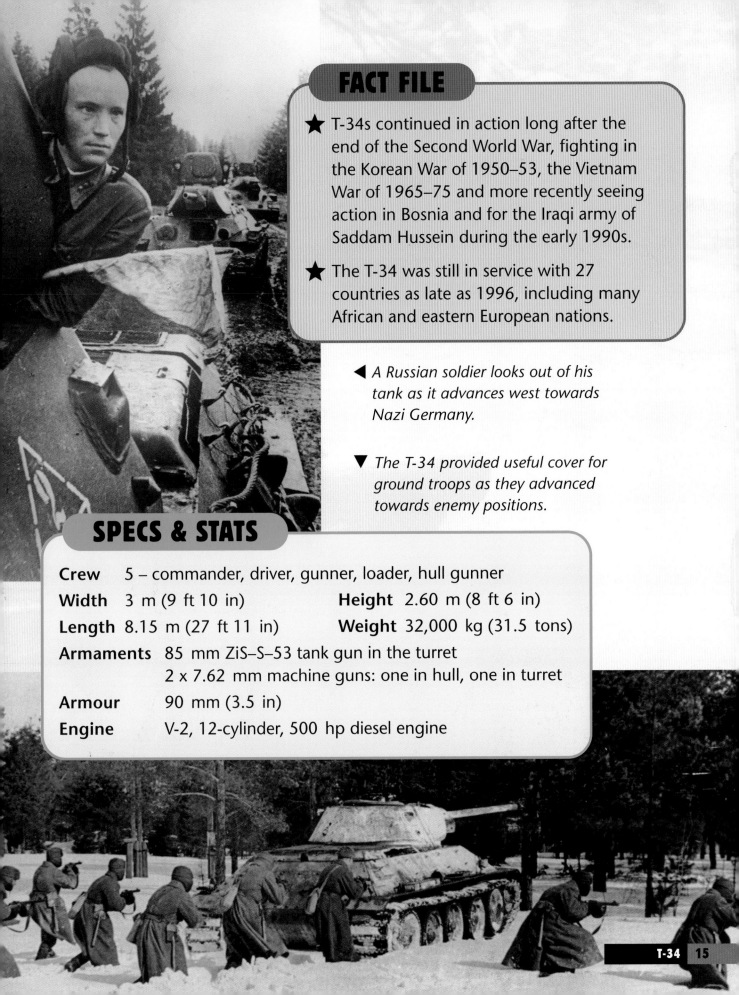

★ T-34s continued in action long after the end of the Second World War, fighting in the Korean War of 1950–53, the Vietnam War of 1965–75 and more recently seeing action in Bosnia and for the Iraqi army of Saddam Hussein during the early 1990s.

★ The T-34 was still in service with 27 countries as late as 1996, including many African and eastern European nations.

◀ A Russian soldier looks out of his tank as it advances west towards Nazi Germany.

▼ The T-34 provided useful cover for ground troops as they advanced towards enemy positions.

SPECS & STATS

Crew   5 – commander, driver, gunner, loader, hull gunner

Width   3 m (9 ft 10 in)   **Height**   2.60 m (8 ft 6 in)

Length 8.15 m (27 ft 11 in)   **Weight**   32,000 kg (31.5 tons)

Armaments   85 mm ZiS–S–53 tank gun in the turret
2 x 7.62 mm machine guns: one in hull, one in turret

Armour   90 mm (3.5 in)

Engine   V-2, 12-cylinder, 500 hp diesel engine

Churchill

The Churchill was a British heavy infantry tank used during the Second World War.

It was named after Winston Churchill, prime minister of Great Britain at the time. He had also been involved with the early development of the tank as a weapon during the First World War.

FACT FILE

★ There were several different versions of the Churchill, including the bridge-laying Ark, the flame-throwing Crocodile, and the armoured recovery vehicle ARV.

★ The Mk IV was almost identical to the earlier Mk III, except that it had a cheaper turret. The Mk V was again almost identical, although it had a 95 mm howitzer in place of the main gun.

A soldier guides a Churchill tank over a scissors bridge: the bridge was carried on top of the tank and was placed to help the tank cross difficult ground.

Improved models

The first version of the Churchill appeared in July 1941 but it had not been tested properly and had an underpowered and unreliable engine and weak armaments. The development of the Mk III and Mk IV in 1942–43 solved these problems. Both versions proved their worth in the invasion of Italy in 1943 and the liberation of western Europe in 1944.

▲ *The powerful engine of later versions of the Churchill allowed it to cross rough ground with ease.*

◄ *Tired foot soldiers hitch a lift on a Churchill as they approach Nijmegen in the Netherlands in September 1944.*

PERFORMANCE

Maximum road speed
24 km/h (15 mph)
Range   90 km (56 miles)

SPECS & STATS

Crew	5 – commander, driver, co-driver/hull gunner, gunner, loader
Width	3 m (10 ft 8 in)
Height	2.8 m (8 ft 2 in)
Length	7.3 m (24 ft 5 in)
Weight	38,500 kg (37.9 tons)
Armaments	QF 6-pdr (57 mm) gun 2 x Besa machine guns
Armour	16–102 mm (0.6–4 in)
Engine	Bedford twin-six, 350 hp petrol engine

M3 Grant

The M3 Medium Tank was the main American tank used in the battle for North Africa against the Germans and Italians in 1942–43.

The British ordered large quantities of the tank, but were unhappy with its high turret and had their own turret fitted that was lower in profile, with a lump at the back for the radio set. These modified tanks were known as Grant tanks, after General Ulysses S Grant who fought in the American Civil War.

▼ *Heavily camouflaged, an M3 tank waits to attack the enemy.*

FACT FILE

★ The main 75 mm gun in the hull could not swivel much in direction, so the whole tank had to turn to face its target when firing.

★ The British called their M3 tanks either Grant, if they were modified, or Lee – after another American Civil War general, Robert E Lee – if they were not. The Americans always called these tanks M3 Mediums.

General Montgomery's tank

The most famous occupant of a Grant tank was General Montgomery, commander of the victorious Eighth Army at the Battle of El Alamein in November 1942. He used his Grant as a command vehicle, but it only had one gun: the 37 mm gun in the turret was in fact a wooden dummy, allowing him more room inside for maps and radio equipment.

◀ *The M3 tank had a low hull and high gun turret, giving it a very distinct profile.*

PERFORMANCE

Maximum road speed	47 km/h (29 mph)
Cross-country speed	40 km/h (25 mph)
Range	275 km (160 miles)

SPECS & STATS

Crew   6 – commander, driver, 2 gunners, 2 loaders

Width   2.7 m (8 ft 11 in)   **Height** 3.1 m (10 ft 3 in)

Length 5.6 m (18 ft 6 in)   **Weight** 28,577 kg (28.1 tons)

Armaments   75 mm gun in the hull, 37 mm gun in the turret

Armour   3.8 cm (1.5 in) maximum

Engine   Twin General Motors 6-71, 375 hp diesel engine

M4A4
Sherman

The M4 Sherman Medium Tank was the main tank produced by the USA during the Second World War.

The tank was named after the famous US General William Sherman and British forces retained this name when they imported the tank for their own use. At least 40,000 Shermans were manufactured.

Service history

The M4 first entered service in North Africa for the British at the Battle of El Alamein in November 1942, and then took part in the US-led invasion of north-west Africa

PERFORMANCE

Maximum road speed
                40 km/h (25 mph)
Cross-country speed
                38.5 km/h (24 mph)
Range   160–240 km (100–150 miles)

It's surprising what a tank will find when it advances into a ruined village!

★ The British nicknamed the first Shermans 'Ronsons' – after the cigarette lighter advertised with the slogan 'Lights up the first time, every time' – because they often exploded at the first hit. The fault was detected in the unprotected ammunition stored just above the tracks. When this was moved, the tanks became much safer.

★ Although the Sherman was inferior in many ways to German or Soviet tanks, it was simple to operate and maintain, was fast and manoeuvrable, and above all was reliable in all conditions.

▲ *Kicking up a cloud of dust, a camouflaged Sherman heads into battle.*

a few weeks later. It continued in service for the rest of the war, and later took part in the Korean War of 1950–53.

▶ *Tank and artillery bombardment wrecked this small French village during the Second World War.*

SPECS & STATS

Crew	5 – commander, gunner, loader, driver, co-driver
Width	2.6 m (8 ft 7 in)
Height	2.7 m (9 ft)
Length	6 m (19 ft 10 in)
Weight	32,205 kg (31.7 tons)
Armaments	75 mm M3 L/40 gun 1 x .50 calibre Browning M2HB machine gun 2 x .30-06 Browning M1919A4 machine guns
Armour	1.3–7.6 cm (0.5–3 in)
Engine	Chrysler A57, multibank petrol engine

Jagdpanther V

The Jagdpanther was a German tank destroyer built in 1944 to 1945. Its name, which means 'hunting panther' in German, was personally chosen by Adolf Hitler, the German leader.

The tank was equipped with a powerful 8.8 cm anti-tank gun. To accommodate this gun, the sides of the tank were extended upwards to provide a roomy interior. Its well-sloped armour made it more likely that enemy shells would ricochet off.

Tank destroyer

About 392 Jagdpanthers were produced in 1944 and 1945. They mainly served on the eastern front against the invading Soviet Red Army. Large numbers were also involved in the Ardennes Offensive – the Battle of the Bulge – fought by the Germans in December 1944 and January 1945 as a last ditch attempt to prevent the Allied invasion of Germany.

The sloping sides of the Jagdpanther deflected enemy shells and gunfire.

FACT FILE

★ The first Allied sighting of the Jagdpanther took place in August 1944, when 12 tanks went into action at the end of the Battle of Normandy to stop the Allied invasion of France.

★ The Jagdpanther was equipped with a powerful 700 hp engine, making it very manoeuvrable on the battlefield.

PERFORMANCE

Maximum road speed 46 km/h (29 mph)
Range   250 km (155 miles)

▼ *The powerful 8.8 cm anti-tank gun gave the Jagdpanther enormous firepower.*

SPECS & STATS

Crew   5 – commander, driver, radio operator, gunner, loader
Width   3.4 m (11 ft 2 in)   **Height** 2.7 m (8 ft 10 in)
Length   6.9 m (22 ft 7 in)   **Weight** 50,150 kg (49.3 tons)
Armaments 1 x 8.8 cm Pak 43/3 or 43/4 L/71 anti-tank gun
              1 x 7.92 mm MG-34 machine gun
Armour   80–100 mm (3–4 in)
Engine   Maybach HL230 P30, V-12, 700 hp petrol engine

Pershing M26

The US Pershing M26 only came into service in February 1945, just as the Second World War was ending.

It was designed as a heavy tank capable of knocking out German tanks up to 2 km (1.2 miles) away and took part in the final assault on Germany.

SPECS & STATS

Crew   5 – commander, driver, co-driver, gunner, loader

Width   3.5 m (11 ft 6 in)   **Height**   2.78 m (9 ft 1 in)

Length 8.65 m (28 ft 5 in)   **Weight**   41,900 kg (41.23 tons)

Armaments   90 mm M3 tank gun
2 x Browning .30-06 machine guns
1 x Browning 12.7 mm machine gun

Armour   25–110 mm (1–4.3 in)

Engine   Ford GAF 8-cylinder, 500 hp petrol engine

A fully loaded Pershing carried 70 shells for its main gun.

PERFORMANCE

Maximum road speed   40 km/h (25 mph)
Range   160 km (100 miles)

FACT FILE

★ The Pershing was named after General John Pershing, who led the American Expeditionary Force that fought in Europe during the First World War.

▲ *This view shows very clearly the low profile and commanding gun turret of the Pershing.*

Korean War

After the war ended, the Pershing was reclassified as a Medium Tank and served in South Korea from 1950–53. Here it was the only tank capable of knocking out the T-34s of the North Korean army. The tank was given a new engine in 1948 and was renamed the M46 General Patton, in honour of one of the most successful US generals of the war.

Chieftain
FV 4201

The Chieftain was the main battle tank of the United Kingdom during the 1960s and 1970s.

The tank was powerfully armed with a 120 mm rifled tank gun and was well protected with heavy armour, although this reduced its overall mobility.

Chieftain models

The first production model – the Chieftain Mk 2 – appeared in 1967. Nine more models appeared until the final Mk 11, equipped with the revolutionary 'Stillbrew' armour and in use with the British army until 1995.

Tank crews trained in the Chieftain in all conditions, advancing through forests and (above) open plains.

FACT FILE

★ Like all British tanks, the Chieftain's name begins with the letter 'C', following on from the Centurion tank and serving alongside the Conqueror heavy tank. It was replaced by the Challenger tank.

★ Chieftains were sold all over the world; the Shah of Iran bought 1,000 before he was overthrown in 1979. His tanks then saw active service in the war against Saddam Hussein's Iraq from 1980–88.

PERFORMANCE

Maximum road speed	48 km/h (25 mph)
Cross-country speed	30 km/h (18.6 mph)
Range	500 km (310 miles)

▲ *Advancing across churned up, muddy ground was no problem for the Chieftain's powerful diesel engine.*

SPECS & STATS

Crew 4 – commander, driver, gunner, loader

Width 3.5 m (11 ft 6 in) **Height** 2.9 m (9 ft 6 in)

Length 7.5 m (24 ft 8 in) **Weight** 55,880 kg (55 tons)

Armaments 120 mm L11A5 rifled tank gun
L8A1 7.62 mm machine gun
L8A1 7.62 mm machine gun mounted on the cupola

Armour Turret: 195 mm (7.7 in), sides 38 mm (1.5 in)

Engine Leyland L60, 750 hp diesel engine

Challenger 1

The Challenger 1 was the main battle tank of the British army from 1983 until Challenger 2 took over after 1998.

The tank is equipped with Chobham armour, a composite armour probably composed of ceramic tiles layered between steel plating, although its exact composition remains a secret.

Gulf War action

In 1991, 180 Challenger tanks took part in the liberation of Kuwait from Iraqi occupation during the Gulf War. The tanks claimed 300 'kills' against armoured vehicles for no losses. One Challenger achieved the longest tank-to-tank kill in military history, destroying an Iraqi tank at a range of 4 km (2.5 miles).

▶ *Two crew members look out through hatches in the top of the hull, while another peeks out under the main gun.*

PERFORMANCE

Maximum road speed	56 km/h (37 mph)
Range	450 km (280 miles)

◀ During the Gulf War in 1991, Challengers hid beneath fine netting covers to camouflage them against the desert sands.

FACT FILE

★ The tank was originally called the Cheviot, after the hills along the English–Scottish border, but it was later renamed the Challenger after a cruiser tank.

★ The Challenger 1 has now been replaced by the Challenger 2, but although they share the same name, the new tank has been completely redesigned and fewer than 5% of its components are interchangeable with its predecessor's.

The Challenger's lengthy tank gun was effective over long distances.

SPECS & STATS

Crew 4 – commander, driver, gunner, loader
Width 3.51 m (11 ft 7 in) **Height** 2.95 m (9 ft 8 in)
Length 8.3 m (27 ft 3 in) **Weight** 62,000 kg (61 tons)
Armaments L11A5 120 mm rifled tank gun
2 x 7.62 mm machine guns
Armour Chobham armour
Engine Rolls-Royce CV12, 26-litre, 1200 hp diesel engine

Glossary

Allies, the
Britain, the USA, France and other countries that fought against Germany and other countries during the First and Second World Wars.

Anti-tank gun
Powerful gun designed to pierce armour and 'kill' or knock out an enemy tank.

Camouflage
Use of paint to conceal the outlines of a tank and thus confuse the enemy.

Chobham armour
Composite armour probably composed of ceramic tiles layered between steel plating. It is named after the British tank research centre at Chobham in Surrey.

Crawler tracks
The endless, jointed metal bands on either side of the tank that are rotated by the engine and enable the tank to move.

Cruiser tank
Light tank designed to operate freely behind enemy lines, cutting lines of supply and communication.

Heavy tank
Heavyweight tank, with strong armour or a powerful gun, now called a battle tank.

Howitzer
Gun designed to fire a heavy shell with a high trajectory or flight-path.

hp
Horsepower, a unit of power.

Hull
Body of the tank.

Hull gunner
Gunner who fires a gun from inside the tank, as opposed to from the turret.

Infantry tank
British heavy tank designed to operate in close co-ordination with infantry soldiers to help them break through enemy lines.

Light tank
Lightweight, lightly armed, highly mobile tank; also called a cruiser tank.

Machine gun
Rapid-firing weapon.

Medium tank
Medium-weight, medium-gunned tank.

Mk
Short for Mark, the model or type of tank.

Panzer
German word for armour.

pdr
Short for pounder, something such as a shell weighing a certain number of pounds.

Tank destroyer
Powerful tank designed to 'kill' or knock out enemy tanks.

Trench
Defensive ditch dug by the armies of both sides during the First World War; an elaborate system of defensive trenches ran along the length of the western front from the English Channel south through Belgium and France to the Swiss border.

Turret
Rotating structure on top of the tank that contains the main gun, as well as room for the commander, gunner, and other crew members.

USSR
Union of Soviet Socialist Republics – a country incorporating Russia, Ukraine and many other republics which existed from 1917–1991. The USSR fought with the Allies during the Second World War.

SOME USEFUL WEBSITES

The Imperial War Museum's official website:
www.iwm.org.uk

The official site of the Tank Museum at Bovington in Dorset:
www.tankmuseum.co.uk/

Wikipedia entries for all the tanks in this book: type in the name of the tank in the Search box and press Go:
http://en.wikipedia.org/wiki/Main_Page

Encyclopedic sites about the two world wars:
www.spartacus.schoolnet.co.uk/FWW.htm
www.spartacus.schoolnet.co.uk/2WW.htm

BBC history sites about the two world wars:
www.bbc.co.uk/history/worldwars/wwone/
www.bbc.co.uk/history/worldwars/wwtwo/

Note to parents and teachers:
Every effort has been made by the Publishers to ensure that the websites in this book are suitable for children, that they are of the highest educational value, and that they contain no inappropriate or offensive material. However, because of the nature of the Internet, it is impossible to guarantee that the contents of these sites will not be altered. We strongly advise that Internet access is supervised by a responsible adult.

Index